THE PATIENT BETTER WORKBOOK

Jennifer Woodruff, MHA

Copyright Information All Rights Reserved.

No portion of this publication may be reproduced, transmitted, or stored in any electronic system in any form or by any means (mechanical, photocopying, electronic, recording or otherwise) without written permission from the author. Brief quotations may be used in literary reviews.

ISBN 13: 978-0-578-62845-5

For Information and bulk ordering:
Email: **orders@PatientBetter.com**
Call in to place an order: 1 (866) 933-2473

www.PatientBetter.com

DISCLAIMER

All content found on the PatientBetter.com Website, Workbook and Handbook, including text, images, audio, templates, or other formats were created for informational purposes only. The content is not intended to be a substitute for professional medical advice, diagnosis, or treatment. Always seek the advice of your licensed health care professional with any questions that you may have regarding a medical condition. Never disregard professional medical advice or delay in seeking it because of something that you have read in the realm of Patient Better's reading material. If you think that you may have a medical emergency, call your practitioner, go to the emergency department, or call 911 immediately. Patient Better does not recommend or endorse any specific tests, physicians, products, procedures, opinions, or other information that may be on Patient Better's handbook or website. Reliance on any information provided by Patient Better handbook, PatientBetter.com, contracted representatives, writers, or medical professionals presenting content for publication to Patient Better is solely at your own risk. All information found on PatientBetter.com Website and Handbook was believed to be correct at the time of inclusion and it is for informational purposes only and not intended as medical advice. References to any treatment or therapy option, or to any program, treatment or service does not constitute official endorsement by Patient Better, Readers are encouraged to fully investigate treatment options and providers that may be more appropriate for specific individuals

TABLE OF CONTENTS

Disclaimer iii

Template and Worksheet Introduction vii

WORKSHEET 1   Contributor Cover Page 1

WORKSHEET 2   Patient Perspective Self-Identification Tool 5

WORKSHEET 3   The Calendar 9

WORKSHEET 4   The Emergency Room Form 13

WORKSHEET 5   The Home Health Care Form 17

WORKSHEET 6   The Medication List 21

WORKSHEET 7   The Durable Medical Equipment Form 25

WORKSHEET 8   The Surgical Form 29

WORKSHEET 9   Research Index Cards 33

WORKSHEET 10   The Chronic Conditions Form 37

WORKSHEET 11   The Patient SOAP Note 41

WORKSHEET 12   The Treatment Plan Calculator 45

Glossary 49

TEMPLATE AND WORKSHEET INTRODUCTION

Patient Better is an educational program that instructs everyday people and their *informal caregivers* how to self-manage care. Today, individuals with medical conditions, and the folks who care for them, are often required to perform high-level medical care in their home. With that being said, it's more critical than ever that these in-home tasks are properly recorded. Patient Better assists patients and their caregivers, parents and guardians how to help keep a good document trail and collaborate care through a user-friendly communication tool.

Patient Better's program is a standard curriculum that educates people through *meaningful learning,* which is a concept where previously learned information is applied and connected to new information. Thus, providing a tool that will align the modern day administrative demands that co-exist with today's health related circumstances.

These templates [worksheets] are an accessory to the program to further the ease of documenting at-home care delivery all while promoting independence through self-health management.

Primary Administration Principles:

1. **Enhance Participation in Treatment:** To have fewer complications, lessen emergency room visits, construct an information-driven medical appointment, and reduce unforeseen costs.

2. **Practice Responsible Medical Utilization:** Prepare for medical appointments, reduce unnecessary phone calls and office visits, and effectively take advantage of offered services, treatment, resources.

3. **Improve Risk Management:** Have a realistic calculation of services needed for proper treatment and recovery to make more informed decisions.

4. **Effectively Self-Manage Care Records:** Become an efficient liaison in the transfer of information from one doctor's office to the next.

Some of this material may seem a bit repetitive. However, you only have to create the framework of the Self-Health Manager once; the rest is just a result of copying, transferring and organizing. It's very important that these worksheets are filled out in its entirety and to the best of your ability. Compose your health history as if you are telling a story as a complete medical autobiography, in your own words, written in your own account.

WORKSHEET 1

CONTRIBUTOR COVER PAGE

Contributor Cover Page: Front and Back

Primary Administration Principles: 3 & 4

FEATURES:

The Contributor Cover Page unites the entire care-giving team. And regardless of assistance capabilities throughout treatment- this worksheet records everyone that participates in the delivery of at-home care. This template helps patients, informal caregivers, parents, and guardians band together as a team, enhance care delivery, and communicate the hierarchy of at-home care giving responsibilities to healthcare professionals.

PURPOSE:

The purpose of this worksheet is to help you develop your at-home care-giving team. The challenge to unify a team, especially on short notice or when in ill-health; is straining. You may find that the contributions of those who participate in your at-home care may be limited. And the limitation lies on the contributor, as they may lack the confidence to deliver care. The Contributor Cover Page is your first qualifier of participation and subtle approach to alleviate the stress of uncertainly.

TIPS FOR USE:

- ✓ Designate a Clearinghouse that can keep up with all Contributors

- ✓ Utilize the Contributor Cover Page and "unearth" additional Contributors that are not regular participants (i.e. if there is a scheduling conflict or as a back-up support)

- ✓ Be sure to include the date on each Contributor Cover Page and it may be revised as often as needed

Patient Better
Contributor Cover Page

Patient Name: _____   D.O.B: ____ / ____ / _____

Primary Clearinghouse:_____

Secondary Clearinghouse:_____

Primary Caregivers: _____

Name: _____   Relationship:_____   Phone:_____

Name:_____   Relationship:_____   Phone:_____

Name: _____   Relationship:_____   Phone:_____

Name:_____   Relationship:_____   Phone:_____

Name:_____   Relationship:_____   Phone:_____

Secondary Caregivers: _____

Company Name:_____

Address:_____

Company Phone:_____   Emergency Phone:_____

Supervisor # 1:_____   Supervisor # 2:_____

Phone:_____   Phone:_____

Secondary Caregivers: _____

Company Name:_____

Address:_____

Company Phone:_____   Emergency Phone:_____

Supervisor # 1:_____   Supervisor # 2:_____

Phone:_____   Phone:_____

Contributor Cover Page

Name (Printed)	Title / Caregiver Relationship	Signature

Contributors:

Healthcare Clearinghouses are considered as the primary overseer(s) of the self-manager. They are the individuals that receive standard information and process it into a non-standard format (from another entity or individual) or vice versa. In most instances, Healthcare Clearinghouses will receive individually identifiable health information only when they have received services from a health care provider, this could also include non-standard information from Primary Caregivers (i.e. family members, friends, and other non-paid caregivers who contribute to the patient's health and well-being) and Secondary Caregivers who are representatives of companies that are paid and typically work in shifts. Secondary caregivers tend to contribute both company-related documentation and Clearinghouse required reports (if needed). Upon signing this Contributor Cover Page, you are in agreement to contribute and report to the best of your ability and as accurately as possible within 24 hours of care-giving and recording it into the self-manager.

WORKSHEET 2

PATIENT PERSPECTIVE SELF-IDENTIFICATION TOOL

SIPP Tool: Front Only

Primary Administration Principles: 3 & 4

FEATURES:

Otherwise known as the "SIPP Tool", you can consider this template as your financial blueprint for condition management. This is your resource to guild you in choosing the best treatment plan to meet financial goals, and to communicate your economic position with your diagnosing office. The SIPP Tool aids in the self-identification and financial philosophies for you and your doctor to create a realistic, obtainable, plan of treatment.

PURPOSE:

The purpose of this worksheet is to provide preliminary financial guidance for you and your contributors when committing to a treatment. The SIPP Tool is used to communicate your analyses (of the financial match) with healthcare professionals. This template allows for quick treatment room decision-making, strengthen money management capabilities, and better align your bank account with treatment costs. If financial management is not thoroughly planned, it may leave you and your family at greater risk to run out of funds half-way through treatment. This worksheet is designed to avoid this from occurring.

TIPS FOR USE:

- ✓ Use the SIPP tool for every treatment plan, as your finances change (and the cost of treatment). Base your decision on the purpose and urgency of the treatment (elective, corrective, exploratory etc.)

- ✓ Use the SIPP Tool with The Treatment Plan Calculator together for each treatment plan

- ✓ Share this tool with every clinician, even if they do not utilize Patient Better's program, you can still utilize this template to summarize your financial position without having to go into detail with every practitioner

Patient Better
Self-Identification Personal Perspective Tool

 The Insurance-Driven Patient	 The Best Practice Patient	 The Rogue Patient	 The Experience-Based Patient
INSURANCE	**RECOMMENDATION**	**CONVENIENCE**	**REPUTATION**
Relies heavily on insurance financing assistance and only seeks care with contracted providers only	Seeks payer assistance whenever possible	Will apply in network payer options when available	This patient type will go abroad if that is the chosen specialist of their desired treatment
Co-creates treatment plan to coincide insurance schedules	Treatment Plans to meet insurance demands, but not limited to in network service providers only	Treatment Plans for payer, convenience, location, and experience that meet treatment goals	Treatment Plans for convenience, location, and reputation
Has an unlimited amount of care options with in-network providers	Has a substantial amount of care options with in-network providers	May have limited payer options, may seek cash pay options if desired care quality is preferred	Seeks care for an experience-based matched provider and does not have insurance

Insurance Driven ←———————————————————————→ Cash Pay

Patient Better © All Rights Reserved | Toll Free: 1 (866) 933-2473 | www.PatientBetter.com

WORKSHEET 3

THE CALENDAR

The Calendar: Front Only

Primary Administration Principles: 1, 2, & 4

FEATURES:

Versatile and unique to Patient Better's self-managing program, created for you and your Contributors to have a reliable scheduling resource. Consider this template as the team's foundation for collaborative independence for any health occurrence. This document is used to aid in time management and schedule coordination of all Care-giving participants. This is a month-long time-management overview that outlines, and forecasts, tasks and events to layout the most complex schedules. The Clearinghouse is responsible for collaborating and copy distribution as well as efficiently track schedules. The Calender is the caregiver's scheduling tool to collaborate with other caregivers and provide a benchmark of long and short-term goals.

PURPOSE:

Not all calendars are designed for healthcare. The Patient Better Calendar is designed specifically for you to maintain a chronological road map of your health. This Calendar unites the entire healthcare team and is available to re-create as many times as you need. And if you notice a discrepancy, no worries, The Calendar is designed to revise and to meet your (or other Contributor's) new schedule demands. Utilize Patient Better's Calendar to assist all Contributors to prioritize, stay on task, time-management, and productivity.

TIPS FOR USE:

- ✓ Designate one person to maintain schedule updates
- ✓ Elect a Clearinghouse that can be the primary schedule communicator
- ✓ Create one "Master" Calendar and then copy and distribute as needed
- ✓ Revise after the month is complete
- ✓ Assign a day for collection or disbursement if others are participatingin a designated spot in the patient's home

Patient Better
Calendar

Patient Name:_____ D.O.B:_____

Created by (Name):_____ Create Date:_____

MONTH:				YEAR:			
PRIMARY DIAGNOSIS:				**DIAGNOSIS DATE:**			
TREATMENT	SUNDAY	MONDAY	TUESDAY	WEDNESDAY	THURSDAY	FRIDAY	SATURDAY
WEEK: ↓							

COMMENTS:

_____

_____

_____

_____

_____

WORKSHEET 4

THE EMERGENCY ROOM FORM

The Emergency Room Form: - Front and Back

Primary Administration Principles: 3 & 4

FEATURES:

The Emergency Room Form provides helpful information to healthcare professionals that normally would take some time to uncover. The Emergency Room Form is also known as a Health Care Proxy Form because it acts as your agent in case you are unable to communicate. Take this worksheet with you wherever you go as it serves healthcare professionals as an accurate directive to your demands (and communicator). For various reasons, people with pre-existing health conditions are three times more likely to wind up in the emergency room.

PURPOSE:

Heaven forbid that you would be in an emergency that would leave you unable to communicate. The Patient Better Emergency Room Form is an in-depth detailer to have on your person at all times. Make this template available to any health professional that you may encounter to secure important information from the unknown.

TIPS FOR USE:

- ✓ Always keep form with you, as it is common knowledge that people are 3 times more likely that you end up in the emergency when health is impaired
- ✓ Complete the Emergency Room form in its entirety
- ✓ Recreate annually or after a visit to the ER

Patient Better
Emergency Form

Last Updated:_____

My Name: (First Last)   D.O.B   Blood Type   Gender
_____ ___/___/___ _____ _____

Religion   Language Spoken   Ethnicity   Phone
_____ _____ _____ _____

Pharmacies:_____
_____
_____
_____

Emergency Contact Person (First Last), Phone #, Relationship, Language Spoke, Email Address

1. _____ _____ _____ _____
2. _____ _____ _____ _____

Current Treating Primary Care Physician (First Last), Facility Name, Location, Phone and Nurse's Name

Dr._____ _____
_____

Medical Conditions (Infections, Allergies, Chronic Condition, State of Condition. & Date Acquired):
_____
_____
_____

Medications and/or Supplements:

_____ _____
_____ _____
_____ _____
_____ _____

Date of last Tetanus shot and Clinic that Administered and ID:
_____

Patient Better Emergency Form

Medical Office Use:

Reason for Emergency Room Visit:

_____
_____

Treating Physician, Name of Facility, Location, Phone Number:

_____
_____

Diagnosis and Treatment:

_____
_____

Service:

_____
_____

Medication:

_____
_____

Follow Up Directions:

_____
_____

WORKSHEET 5

THE HOME HEALTH CARE FORM

The Home Health Care (Analysis and Interview) Form: Front and Back

Primary Administration Principles: 2 & 3

FEATURES:

This worksheet is designed for you to find the right home service provider- the first time around. This mutual resume is interactive and is a reliable guide to match your needs to the home health care services' offering. Tutorial found in Section 2 Article 2 Titled: "Home Health and Home Care Services".

PURPOSE:

One of the greatest challenges is finding a Home Health or Home Care center that matches your unique needs. If you are lucky enough, you will have a trusted home health facility in your community or have a referral from your doctor's office. Without these conveniences, people are more at-risk to not finding the right facility (and this could happen for various reasons). Write your specifications for each company on the back of the worksheet. By doing this you will better analyze and communicate your necessities and expectations to either the home health and/or home care center, and find the right representative or professional to come to your home- the first time.

TIPS FOR USE:

- ✓ Print this out for every company, representative, or professional

- ✓ Include the company's representatives into The Calendar and The Treatment Plan Calculator if that is your demands and share the Patient Better Program as needed

- ✓ Use this worksheet as a self-examination to identify desired tasks to match the right representative to the skill requirement

Home Care Chart

Patient Name:_____ D.O.B:_____ Create Date:_____

Is this care prescribed as medical necessity and part of a treatment plan? Yes No

What is the name of the primary diagnosis and primary ICD code associated with home care necessity?

1. Diagnosis _____ ICD:_____

2. Diagnosis:_____ ICD:_____

3. Diagnosis:_____ ICD:_____

Type of care (Circled):

Home Health Care (Medical)   Personal Assistive Care

Home Care (non-medical)   Rehabilitative Care (Therapeutic)

Company Name: _____

Type of care: _____

Supervisor: _____

Office Phone:_____ Office Hours:_____

Off Hours Phone Number:_____

Address: _____

Email: _____ Website: _____

Company Name: _____

Type of care: _____

Supervisor: _____

Office Phone:_____ Office Hours:_____

Off Hours Phone Number:_____

Address: _____

Email: _____ Website: _____

Service expectations for company #1:

___

Service expectations for company #2:

___

Comments:

WORKSHEET 6
THE MEDICATION LIST

The Medication (and Supplement) Form: Front Only

Primary Administration Principles: 2 & 3

FEATURES:

Not all Medications are alike. The in-depth tutorial is found in Section 2 Article 3 Titled: "Prescription Medications" that explains how vital your account of actual use is. Research shows that the prescriber can only assume that you have picked up medication and were compliant. Use The Medication List Form, not as a duplicate from of the pharmacy, but as proof that you have followed the doctor's direction. This form is to track actual usage and incorporate all medications and supplements and as a one-source documenter. If there is not a pharmacy- put the place where you got the supplement such as "GNC" or "Amazon.com". So far, this is the best communicator we have on the market to show providers your compliance and commitment to following the treatment plan.

PURPOSE:

"According to the Center for Disease Control and Prevention (CDC), only 50% of prescribed medication is filled [and of that] only 30% of that medication is taken properly." However, the prescriber has [no other choice] to assume that you took the medication properly and to its entirety [unless otherwise specified]. If you feel uncomfortable in any way with the treatment plan that the doctor ordered; by all means, this worksheet is your tool to bring up your concerns (try a different regime or discuss possible alternatives).

TIPS FOR USE:

- ✓ Document the manufacturer and lot number tracking (for recall purposes) and save the packaging in Self-Health Manager pocket labeled "MEDS"

- ✓ Assign each pharmacy number on the "peach colored box" (left side of form) even if you only have one pharmacy- so that people can quickly identify your over the counter medication in instances when you obtain all therapies in one retail location such as Walgreen's or Walmart

- ✓ Once completed, document that you have finished the medication; if left blank, it is understood that you are 1. Still taking the medication 2. Not compliant (so you need a reason why you did not take it as prescribed)

Patient Better
Medication Form

Patient Name: _____ D.O.B: _____

PRESCRIBER	MEDICATION & LOT #	STRENGTH	UNIT DOSE	TIMES A DAY	PRIMARY DIAGNOSIS ICD	START DATE	END DATE	KNOWN DRUG INTERACTIONS

Pharmacy #

Pharmacy Name:
Phone Number:
Address:
City, State, Zip:

Pharmacy #

Pharmacy Name:
Phone Number:
Address:
City, State, Zip:

Pharmacy #

Pharmacy Name:
Phone Number:
Address:
City, State, Zip:

WORKSHEET 7
THE DURABLE MEDICAL EQUIPMENT FORM

The Durable Medical Equipment Form: Front Only

Primary Administration Principles: 2 & 3

FEATURES:

With all the Durable Medical Equipment companies out there, locating the right one is more important than ever. Find a qualified company to get exactly what the doctor prescribed quick-ly. Tutorial found in Section 2 Article 4 Titled: "Durable Medical Equipment (DME)".

PURPOSE:

As medicine evolves, durable medical equipment approval(s) will continue to change. Other variables will factor into DME accessibility as well. Occasionally, manufacturer representatives may live far away from the immediate scope of the healthcare system or may be prescribed an unusual device. Utilize this form to help you gage the time and cost of the ever changing DME approval and to build a better relationship with those involved in your equipment.

TIPS FOR USE:

- ✓ Equipment can be an extremely useful tool to use throughout therapy, (if used correct-ly) make sure that you have the instructions handy in the Self-Health Manager's pocket labeled "DME"

- ✓ Place all the durable medical equipment's documentation and the representative's information in the pocket behind the tab labeled "DME" in the Self-Health Manager

- ✓ Be sure to visit article 2.4 Durable Medical Equipment in your Patient Better User Guide prior to getting an approved and then later denied claim reversed

Patient Better
Durable Medical Equipment Information

Referring Physician: _____

Date of Referral: _____

ICD Codes: _____

Medical Device Name: _____

Primary Function: _____

Manufacturer: _____

Physical Address: _____

Company Phone #: _____

Model Number: _____

Date beginning use of device: _____ Date _____

Did you receive the device in a timely manner?	Yes	No
Did you feel that you were properly educated your device?	Yes	No
Was the company informative about their billing?	Yes	No

Did you have a medical device company representative come to your home or meet you at your place of healthcare?   Yes   No

If Yes

Name of Representative

First and last name   Contact Number

_____   _____

Was your representative they friendly, presented the company well, and informative about the steps going through the ordering process?   Yes   No

Did you receive you device in the mail?   Yes   No

If Yes

Were you informed properly on how to use the device through educational material such as YouTube videos, company websites or modules and DVD/CDs.?   Yes   No

Please give a detailed review of 100 words or more of your experience with your device:

_____

_____

_____

_____

WORKSHEET 8

THE SURGICAL FORM

The Surgical Form: Front and Back

Primary Administration Principles: 2 & 3

FEATURES:
Used to record identification numbers and all surgical service provider's information and affiliations. Used as a forever-record to track recalls and safety alerts from the manufacturer throughout time.

PURPOSE:
There are many reasons to have surgery. Some operations can relieve or prevent pain. Others can reduce a symptom of a problem or improve body function. Some surgeries are performed to find a problem. Nevertheless, all surgeries should be well documented. You can consider this Surgical Form as your tracking tool to record a day in your life that you would have otherwise forgotten.

TIPS FOR USE:
- ✓ Form belongs in the pocket behind the tab labeled "SURG"
- ✓ Include implants, device numbers and Identification Cards
- ✓ Document all surgeries, including inpatient, outpatient, or elective

Surgical Form

Name:_____ Date:_____

Original Diagnosis date:_____ Primary ICD Code(s):_____

Surgery Information:

Surgery Center Name: _____ Phone:_____

Address: _____ City: _____ Zip:_____

Date of Surgery: _____ Name of Surgery:_____R L B

Surgeon Information

Name: _____ Phone: _____

Primary Address: _____ City: _____ Zip:_____

Contact Person (First and Last Name):_____

Surgical Device Information #1

Name of Device: _____ Tracking ID:_____

Manufacturer:_____ Phone:_____

Address:_____ City: _____ Zip:_____

Location: _____   Right   Left

Surgical Device Information #2

Name of Device: _____ Tracking ID:_____

Manufacturer:_____ Phone:_____

Address:_____ City: _____ Zip:_____

Location: _____   Right   Left   Both

Post-Surgical Treatment Plan: _____
_____
_____
_____
_____
_____

Surgery Support Team:

Home Health Agency: _____	Phone: _____
Contact Name: _____	Cell: _____
Skilled Facility Name: _____	Phone: _____
Contact Name: _____	Cell: _____
Therapy Center Name: _____	Phone: _____
Contact Name: _____	Cell: _____
Other Name: _____	Phone: _____
Contact Name: _____	Cell: _____

Outcome Overview (include primary provider name, shared outcome, & date):
_____
_____
_____
_____

ADDITIONAL NOTES:
_____
_____
_____
_____
_____
_____

WORKSHEET 9
RESEARCH INDEX CARDS

Research Index Cards: Front Only

Primary Administration Principles: 2, 3 & 4

FEATURES:
Show your provider that you are invested and interested in your healthcare. Document your research and bring your findings back to your provider to authenticate your discovery and ensure that you will get a professionally researched answer to your query. In-depth tutorial found in Section 3 Article 7 Titled: "Research Smart".

PURPOSE:
These cards are there for your disposal and for you to capture all of your medical curiosities. Today's healthcare professional understands that their patients often conduct research on the web before an office visit. Today's clinician expects their patients to be more forthcoming and involved in their care as well as feel more comfortable to openly discuss findings. These cards are designed for you to use to organize your interests and discoveries in a uniform presentation.

TIPS FOR USE:
- ✓ Look for current, unbiased information
- ✓ Preform a check in websites in the "About Us" page
- ✓ Use cards to document any communication channel. Books, magazines and newspapers include the page number and location if necessary

Patient Better
Research Index Cards

Website/Magazine/Commercial:
Company/Organization:
The writer's information:
Date that you found the issue:
The date that the issue was published:

- -

Website/Magazine/Commercial:
Company/Organization:
The writer's information:
Date that you found the issue:
The date that the issue was published:

- -

Website/Magazine/Commercial:
Company/Organization:
The writer's information:
Date that you found the issue:
The date that the issue was published:

- -

Website/Magazine/Commercial:
Company/Organization:
The writer's information:
Date that you found the issue:
The date that the issue was published:

WORKSHEET 10

THE CHRONIC CONDITIONS

Chronic Conditions Form: Front and Back

Primary Administration Principles: 1, 3 & 4

FEATURES:

Recollection of chronic condition onset while in the treatment room- is simply not enough. Fill this template out before your office visit and provide a quick snapshot of the condition(s), onset, and current treatment regimen to save you and your service provider a significant amount of time. By completing this form you will pave the way for a more information-driven appointment. An in-depth tutorial found in Section 3 Article 6 Titled: "Chronic Conditions and the American Payout". This worksheet is designed for you to "pick up where you left off" meaning that if you have neglected condition and you have found the right specialist, the Chronic Conditions Form is the perfect guide to document your health journey. The backside of this worksheet is for you and your professional to start collaborating an active plan of treatment- today!

PURPOSE:

According to the CDC, the leading causes of death and disability as well as the leading drivers to the nation's $3.5 Trillion annual healthcare costs- are chronic conditions. Six out of ten adults have a chronic condition and 4 out of 10 have 2 chronic conditions or more. This worksheet frees up the valuable treatment room time recalling your condition(s) and allows for a quick assessment and advance in a more in-depth evaluation. This is a mid-level worksheet is designed for chronic conditions that have been previously diagnosed.

TIPS FOR USE:

- ✓ Fill out the form to the best of your ability

- ✓ Copy the information if you need to update the worksheet and share it will every professional

- ✓ Don't throw this Chronic Condition From away after use, instead, put it in your Specialty pocket behind label "SPC"

Chronic Care Management Form

Patient Name: _____ DOB: _____

Document Prepared By: _____ Date: _____

Condition:	
Date Diagnosed:	
The Diagnosing Clinician's Name:	
Diagnosing Clinician's Address/Phone:	
How was onset determined?	
ICD codes associated with the condition:	
Did the clinician refer a specialist?	
Specialist's Name and Specialty:	
Specialist's Address/Phone:	
Meds associated with this condition:	
Comments:	

Condition:	
Date Diagnosed:	
The Diagnosing Clinician's Name:	
Diagnosing Clinician's Address/Phone:	
How was onset determined?	
ICD codes associated with the condition:	
Did the clinician refer a specialist?	
Specialist's Name and Specialty:	
Specialist's Address/Phone:	
Meds associated with this condition:	
Comments:	

Condition:	
Date Diagnosed:	
The Diagnosing Clinician's Name:	
Diagnosing Clinician's Address/Phone:	
How was onset determined?	
ICD codes associated with the condition:	
Did the clinician refer a specialist?	
Specialist's Name and Specialty:	
Specialist's Address/Phone:	
Meds associated with this condition:	
Comments:	

Chronic Care Management Form

Treatment Plan Option Overview (See Treatment Plan Calculator):

Condition:_____ ICD Codes:_____

Option Title 1:_____ Start Date:_____ Projected Duration:_____

Option Title 2:_____ Start Date:_____ Projected Duration:_____

Option Title 3:_____ Start Date:_____ Projected Duration:_____

Special Reminders (Wait for clearance, follow treatment plan, contribute to outcome):

_____
_____
_____
_____
_____
_____

Clinic Support Notes:

_____
_____
_____
_____
_____
_____

Outcome Overview:_____

NOTES:

_____
_____
_____
_____

WORKSHEET 11
THE PATIENT SOAP NOTE

The Patient SOAP Note: Front and Back

Primary: Administration Principles: 1, 2, 3 & 4

FEATURES:

This worksheet is the core centerpiece of the Patient Better program. Used for recording all concerns and occurrences in-between office visits. Use this worksheet to capture pertinent in-formation regarding specific issues and incidences. Provide this form to applicable providers in the most widely used format of note taking by professionals. Fill out a SOAP Note for each provider visit. This in-depth tutorial for creation is found in Section 5 Article 1 Titled: "Writing, Organizing, and Keeping Notes and Records".

PURPOSE:

The purpose of The SOAP Note is to better the productivity in your office visit. The goal of this strategic worksheet is to document all of your concerns and address them while in the treatment room to reduce additional office visits and unnecessary phone calls.

TIPS FOR USE:

- ✓ To better prepare and be more productive in the treatment room
- ✓ Use for strategic treatment planning
- ✓ Use as an outline and overview of occurrences
- ✓ Create a SOAP Note for each provider, (i.e. Woman's wellness, post-surgical checkups) and create a follow-up SOAP Note as a continuum for each appointment

MENTIONS:

When writing your SOAP Note (right hand side under "Issues") give providers a "needs-to-know" snap-shot of the reason(s) why you came to their office. Include the immediate incident and the symptoms of the Primary Mention- (When did it start?) Location - (Where is it located?), Duration (How long has it been going on?), Severity (How bothersome or disruptive is it?). Secondary Mentions (Why did the onset start?)the severity and ow long has the onset been going on. Be sure to include the(day & time) incident and document whether it gradual, or did it happen quickly or if the onset may have been a predecessor of another issue.

Puss	Wheezing
Inflamed	Shortness of breath
Swelling	Aching
Burn	Bruising (how many days after the trauma did it appear)
Tingling	
Pain	Productive cough
Experience pain while…	Sore
Sharp pain	Tender
Dull pain	Infected
Hurts when touched	Size and Shape
Cramp	Place that it happened
Numb	Colors (red, green, white)
Bleeding (for how long)	Mild
Feverish	Severe
Dizzy	Lingering
Coughing	Unexpected
Congested	Reoccurring
Pounding/throbbing	Annoying
Dry cough	Constant

Patient Better
Patient-Prepared S.O.A.P. Note

Created by (Name):_____ Create Date:_____

Patient First Name:_____ Last Name:_____

First time at this clinic: Yes   No   Date of Birth:_____

Who/Where referred: Issues that I have been having:
_____
                                              Issue #1
Why I am here today: Start Date:
_____   Location
_____   Duration
_____   Severity
_____   Comments:

Previously diagnosed Chronic Conditions and date of diagnosis:
                                              Issue #2
_____   Start Date:
_____   Location
_____   Duration
_____   Severity
                                              Comments:

Medications and supplements that I took since last visit overview (name, dosage, and start-end date):
                                              Issue #2
_____   Start Date:
_____   Location
_____   Duration
_____   Severity
                                              Comments:

Some notable events that happened since my last appointment:
                                              Issue #2
_____   Start Date:
_____   Location
_____   Duration
_____   Severity
_____   Comments:

Patient-Prepared S.O.A.P. Note

Diagnosis: _____ ICD: _____ Date: _____

Diagnosis: _____ ICD: _____ Date: _____

Treatment Plan Options Overview: (See Attachments or Self-Manager):

_____
_____
_____
_____
_____
_____

Special Instructions (Wait for clearance, follow treatment plan, contribute to outcome):

_____
_____
_____
_____

Clinic Support Staff:

_____
_____
_____
_____

Outcome Overview (Overall experience, cost calculation accuracy, and commitment to treatment):

_____
_____
_____
_____

Additional Notes:

_____
_____
_____
_____
_____

WORKSHEET 12
THE TREATMENT PLAN CALCULATOR

The Treatment Plan Calculator: Front Only

Primary Administration Principles: 1, 3, & 4

FEATURES:

In the instance when users have two or more options of therapy, the Treatment Calculator helps project the manpower and costs on both the large and small scales. This high-level worksheet forecasts participation of who can deliver at-home care within a projected time. The Treatment Plan Calculator is the perfect companion to the Contributor Cover Page, the Calendar, and the SIPP Tool and provides invaluable insight into upcoming expenses, overall treatment costs, and ability to evaluate who would be the best contributor to assign to any given task.

PURPOSE:

The purpose of this worksheet is to help users determine the most financially feasible treatment plan possible. When applied with other worksheets, users can pinpoint contributor's participation abilities and estimate commitment necessities. Moreover, this adaptable template can be enforced in any given time in treatment allowing for a heightened patient experience and further projection of direct and indirect expenditures. The in-depth tutorial found in Section 5 Article 2 Titled: "Treatment Planning".

TIPS FOR USE:

- ✓ Identify schedule conflicts with The Calendar

- ✓ Treatment Plan Calculator should be revisited every 6 weeks to 3 months as some points of time in treatment are more demanding and may have more schedule conflicts

- ✓ Jot down at least 3 Pros and 3 Cons of each initial treatment possibility

Patient Better
Treatment Plan Calculator

Patient Name:_____ D.O.B._____

Created by (Name): _____ Date Created:_____

Option #_____	Title:_____			Total Annual Deductible			
Projected Length of Time:_____				Ins. Coverage $_____			
DOCTOR VISITS		EVERY	DD / WK / MO / YR	Y	N	OOP:	$
MEDICATION		EVERY	DD / WK / MO / YR	Y	N	OOP:	$
DIAGNOSTIC IMAGING		EVERY	DD / WK / MO / YR	Y	N	OOP:	$
LAB TESTS		EVERY	DD / WK / MO / YR	Y	N	OOP:	$
SURGERY		EVERY	DD / WK / MO / YR	Y	N	OOP:	$
THERAPY		EVERY	DD / WK / MO / YR	Y	N	OOP:	$
EQUIPMENT		EVERY	DD / WK / MO / YR	Y	N	OOP:	$
IN-HOME CARE		EVERY	DD / WK / MO / YR	Y	N	OOP:	$

PROJECTED HOURS: _____ EVERY DD / WK / MO / YR   Total: $_____

PROS **CONS**

_____ _____
_____ _____
_____ _____
_____ _____
_____ _____
_____ _____
_____ _____

COMMENTS:

_____
_____
_____
_____
_____
_____
_____

GLOSSARY

Fee for Service Medical Practice (FFS): Is a traditional payment model within clinics where services are unbundled and paid for separately. In health care, it gives an incentive for physicians to provide more treatments because payment is dependent on the quantity of care, rather than quality of care.

Informal Caregivers: Are referred to by clinicians as the friends and family of the patient who are uncompensated and have no prior formal health training and are delivering daily at-home care (most common examples are spouses, family members, neighbors, co-workers, and friends).

Meaningful Learning (ML): Refers to the concept that previously learned knowledge is fully understood by the individual and that the individual knows how that specific information relates to other stored data (stored in your brain that is) and is applied to the newly learned material. For understanding this concept, it is good to contrast meaningful learning with the much less desirable, rote learning.

Relationship-Centered Care (RCC): is a framework for conceptualizing health care which recognizes that the nature and quality of relationships in health care influence the process and outcomes of health care. An extension of Patient -Centered Care, relationship-centered care is founded upon four principles: (1) that relationships in health care ought to include the person-hood of the participants, (2) that affect and emotion are important components of these relationships, (3) that all health care relationships occur in the context of reciprocal influence, and (4) that the formation and maintenance of relationships in care participation is morally valuable.

Patient-Centered Care: Involves individual patients in their specific care demands. The IOM (Institute of Medicine) defines patient-centered care as: "Providing care that is respectful of, and responsive to, individual patient preferences, needs and values, and ensuring that patient values guide all clinical decisions."

Pay for Performance Medical Practice (P4P): In the healthcare industry, pay for performance (P4P), also known as "value-based purchasing", is a payment model that offers financial incentives to physicians, hospitals, medical groups, and other healthcare providers for meeting certain performance measures.

Value Based Medicine: Global healthcare in the 21st century is characterized by evidence-based medicine (EBM), patient-centered care, and cost effectiveness. EBM involves clinical decisions being made by integrating patient preference with medical treatment evidence and physician experiences. The Center for Value-Based Medicine suggested value-based medicine (VBM) as the practice of medicine based upon the patient-perceived value conferred by an intervention. VBM starts with the best evidence-based data and converts it to patient value-based data, so that it allows clinicians to deliver higher quality patient care than EBM alone. The final goals of VBM are improving quality of healthcare and using healthcare resources efficiently.

www.ingramcontent.com/pod-product-compliance
Lightning Source LLC
Chambersburg PA
CBHW081156290426
44108CB00018B/2579